D1712894

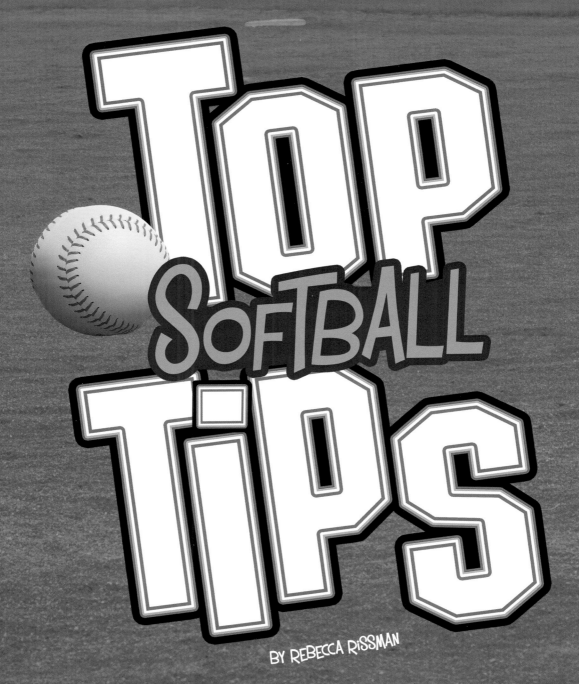

TOP SOFTBALL TIPS

BY REBECCA RISSMAN

CAPSTONE PRESS

Snap Books are published by Capstone Press
1710 Roe Crest Drive, North Mankato, Minnesota 56003
www.mycapstone.com

Library of Congress Cataloging-in-Publication Data is available on the Library of Congress website.

ISBN 978-1-5157-4721-5 (library hardcover)
ISBN 978-1-5157-4727-7 (paperback)
ISBN 978-1-5157-4745-1 (eBook PDF)

Summary: Learn the basics and the tips for playing softball.

EDITORIAL CREDITS

Editor: Gena Chester
Designer: Veronica Scott
Media Researcher: Eric Gohl
Production Specialist: Kathy McColley

PHOTO CREDITS

Capstone Studio: Karon Dubke, 10, 12, 13 (all); iStockphoto: filo, 17, Iris Nieves, 20 (bottom), Motionshooter, 18 (bottom); Newscom: Cal Sport Media/Erik Williams, 19, Xinhua News Agency/ Ye Pingfan, 4, ZUMA Press/Damon Higgins, 27, ZUMA Press/Daniel Wallace, 29 (bottom), ZUMA Press/David Joles, 11, ZUMA Press/Douglas R. Clifford, 8, ZUMA Press/Greg Sorber, 7, 26, ZUMA Press/Jon-Michael Sullivan, 23, ZUMA Press/Keith Birmingham, 22, ZUMA Press/Lance Aram Rothstein, 9; Shutterstock: Jan de Wild, 5, 15, 16, 21, 24, 29 (top), Mega Pixel, cover (bat), Mejini Neskah, cover (ball), 1, 6 (top), 18 (top), 20 (top), 32, Nicholas Piccillo (field background), Opka, 6 (bottom), Wendy Nero, 25

Printed and bound in Canada
10040S17FR

TABLE OF CONTENTS

Chapter 1

COVERING
Your Bases

The story of softball goes all the way back to a hot gymnasium in 1887. A group of college football fans were anxiously waiting to hear the results of a game between Yale and Harvard.

When Yale won, the crowd erupted in cheers. A Yale fan picked up a stray boxing glove and threw it at a Harvard fan. Instead of dodging the glove, the Harvard fan tried to hit it with a long stick! Before long, the football score was forgotten and the first softball game had begun.

The Basics

Softball is a bat-and-ball sport played between two 9-player teams. Each game is divided into **innings**. Most games are seven innings long. Sometimes at the end of seven innings, both teams will have a tie. To break a tie, games go into extra innings. They continue for one, two, or even three additional innings until one team has a higher score.

Softball is played on a diamond-shaped field. The infield is covered in dirt. At the center of the infield is the pitcher's mound. The outfield is the grass-covered area behind the infield.

inning—a period in a softball game; each team has the chance to field balls and bat once during an inning

Take the Field

There are nine different fielding positions in softball. The left fielder, center fielder, and right fielder are all outfield positions. These players are excellent runners and have strong throwing arms. They are responsible for catching or fielding any balls that are hit past the infield.

Infield positions include first baseman, second baseman, shortstop, and third baseman. These players are quick on their feet and throw fast with great precision. They must field any balls hit into the infield. Infielders are also responsible for tagging base runners and covering their bases.

The last two infield positions are the pitcher and catcher. The pitcher throws the ball for the batter on the opposite team to try to hit. The catcher catches and returns any pitches that aren't hit. She is also in charge of guarding home plate and throwing out runners on bases.

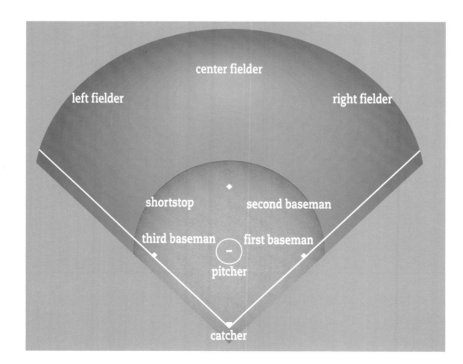

In a League of Your Own

The best way to improve your softball skills is to join a league. There are many different types of softball leagues. Some are associated with schools. The girls on these teams are all from the same school. Community organizations form other leagues. These are usually less competitive than school leagues. Usually, the competitive leagues are private. Players from around the **region**, along with local players, can participate in private leagues.

Competitive leagues require players to try out. This means the players need to display some of their softball skills, such as hitting, throwing, and catching. They do this to show the coaches their strengths and weaknesses. Tryouts help coaches find the right players for each team.

region—an area or district

TRAIN *to Win*

Softball requires strength, flexibility, and **endurance**. To make sure that they're ready to win, softball players work on physical **conditioning** before their season starts.

Stretch!

Try these simple stretches to keep your muscles flexible and healthy.

FORWARD FOLD: From a standing position, keep a slight bend in your knees. Bend forward at the waist while reaching for your toes.

SHOULDER STRETCH: Bring your right arm across your chest. Pull it closer with your left arm or hand so you feel the stretch. Switch arms.

WRIST ROLLS: Hold a softball in each hand. Extend your arms straight out in front of you and make circles with each ball. Roll only your wrists. Change directions.

Run for it!

Cardiovascular exercises challenge the heart and lungs, helping to keep players in tiptop shape. Running is a great cardio activity for softball players. These types of runs will prepare you for softball practice.

ENDURANCE RUNS: Before your season starts, build endurance by taking long runs. Run for 20 minutes every other day.

SPRINT: Build your speed and agility by sprinting from home base to first and back again. Take a 60 second break, and do it again. Then take a 50 second break, and sprint again. Decrease your rest time by 10 seconds every time. Once you make it to 0 seconds, you're done!

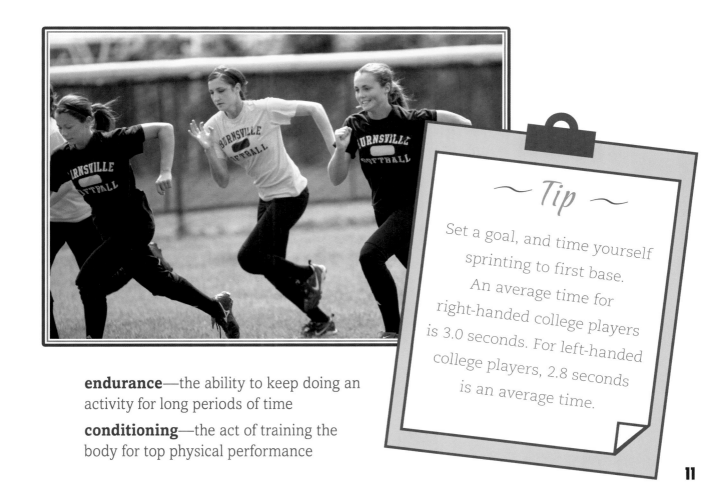

~ *Tip* ~

Set a goal, and time yourself sprinting to first base. An average time for right-handed college players is 3.0 seconds. For left-handed college players, 2.8 seconds is an average time.

endurance—the ability to keep doing an activity for long periods of time

conditioning—the act of training the body for top physical performance

Strength Training

Softball players need to build strong muscles in order to succeed on the field. Strength training workouts build muscular health so that players can hit harder and throw farther.

Upper-Body Work

A-Z SHOULDER WORK: With tape, mark a square 1 foot (0.3 meters) wide and 1 foot (0.3 m) tall on the wall. The square should be at shoulder height. Stand back from the wall so that your fingertips barely touch it when your arms are straight out. Starting with your right hand's pointer finger in the middle of the box with your arm out straight, draw the alphabet using only your shoulder. Switch arms. Repeat until each arm has done this four times.

Lower Body Work

SQUATS: Stand with your feet shoulder-width apart or slightly wider and your toes pointing forward. Bend your knees deeply, then stand back up. Keep weight on the heels of your feet instead of your toes. Do 20 repetitions three times.

Core Work

LEG LIFTS: Switch up your sit ups! Try doing sit ups with your legs lifted, lowered, and straight. Start with your entire body on the ground, lying on your back. Keeping your legs together and straight, slowly lift your legs up so that your body makes a 90 degree angle. Slowly lower your legs, keeping your feet about 6 inches (15 centimeters) from the ground. Repeat the lift. For added difficulty, raise your hips off the ground as your legs lift up.

~ Tip ~

Start at 10 or 12 leg lifts per set. Then add in one or two repetitions per set, per week. Keep it up until you can do three sets of 20.

Chapter 3

BATTER Up

Training to hit the ball out of the park means learning to hit the ball hard. Softball players do strength-training workouts to increase their batting power. They also add sport-specific workouts, focusing on hand-eye coordination, timing, and accuracy.

Batting Mechanics

Good hitters practice proper batting mechanics every day for great hits. Square your shoulders to home plate and have your feet at least shoulder-distance apart. Grip the bat gently with both hands and line up your second set of knuckles. Before you start your swing, take a small step, or trigger step, toward the pitcher with your front foot. Keep your weight back on the inside of your back foot. Start your swing by slightly shifting your hips, legs, and weight toward the pitcher. At the same time, bring the knob of your bat towards the ball, keeping your front shoulder in. Snap your wrists through to swing your bat head around and make contact with the ball. The ball should hit the bat in the middle of its barrel. Let the force of your swing open your hips and shoulders to the pitcher.

~ Tip ~

Keep your eyes on the ball the whole time! Batters should watch the pitcher's hip during her circle motion. Once the ball is at her hip and leaves her fingers, track the ball all the way until it makes contact with your bat.

HITTING *Colors*

Batters need to think on their toes. They must wait until the very last second to decide if a pitch is in the strike zone. This drill helps players develop the speed and agility needed to take their hitting game to the next level.

Have a friend hold two different colored softballs. Using an underhand toss, she throws both balls to your **strike zone** at the same time. After releasing them, she calls out one color. Hit whichever color she calls out. Don't have colored balls? Have your partner call out top or bottom ball instead.

strike zone—the imaginary box in a batter's hitting zone that determines whether a pitch is a ball or a strike; usually located above the knees and below the chest on a batter

Base Running Basics

Running the bases might seem simple, but it's actually a very **strategic** skill softball players need to master. After all, they can't score without making it to home plate. To be fast and efficient, players do a lead off. As soon as the pitcher releases the ball, players run a few feet away from the base. Runners can't be too far away. They need to make it back quickly in case the catcher tries to throw them out. While running the bases, players always watch the ball so that they know whether to **round** a base or stop on it.

Stealing Mechanics

Want to test your opponents and your speed? Steal! Stand on the balls of your feet with your knees bent and keep your eye on the pitcher. As soon as she releases the ball, take off! Run hard and fast to the next base. If you beat the tag, you're safe!

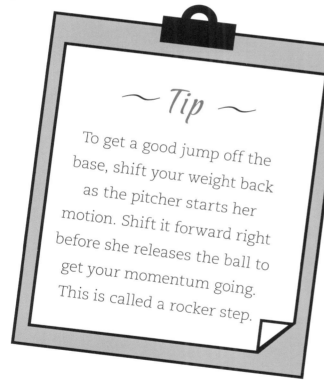

~ Tip ~

To get a good jump off the base, shift your weight back as the pitcher starts her motion. Shift it forward right before she releases the ball to get your momentum going. This is called a rocker step.

strategy—a plan for winning a competition

round—to approach the base at a curved angle, step on the inside corner of the base, and take a couple of steps off the base to see where the ball is

momentum—the force or speed created by movement

BE SAFE, *Slide*

Any time a play looks close at second base, third base, or home plate, slide! Sliding makes it harder for a fielder to tag you with the ball. Start your slide when you're about four steps away from the base. Bring your weight into your left side. Bend your left leg and tuck it behind your right to make a "4." As you do this, lean back and let your **momentum** carry you to the ground. The speed of your sprint should propel your body feet first into the base.

Bunt!

Not all softball players step up to the plate hoping to hit one over the fences. For some situations, they need to bunt. Bunters try to make the ball travel as short a distance as possible. The infielders must scramble forward to get the ball, giving the batter and other runners time to get to the next base.

Sacrifice Bunt Mechanics

Sometimes, a batter needs to help her teammate advance to the next base. The batter gives up her chance to hit the ball and instead does a sacrifice bunt.

Start in the front of the box in your regular batting stance. Soon after the pitcher starts her motion, pivot to turn your hips and shoulders toward the pitcher. Bring your weight to your front foot, and drop your back knee toward the ground. Slightly bend into your front knee. Quickly bring the bat around so that it is toward the pitcher. Hold the bat parallel to the ground. Slide your bottom hand toward the knob of the bat. Bring your top hand to the beginning of the barrel. Tuck your fingers underneath, and curl your thumb around the bat. Practice these steps until you can do them in one smooth motion. And remember, only bunt strikes!

~ Tip ~

Are you super speedy? Then try a surprise bunt! The only difference from a sacrifice bunt is timing. Players move into their bunt position after the ball has left the pitcher's hand. This catches the infielders by surprise and allows fast sprinters to reach first before the defense can get to the ball.

RING AROUND
the Home Plate

This drill will help players learn to keep their bunts close to home plate. The key to this drill is having "soft hands." Don't poke! Instead, let the ball come to you and act as if the bat could catch it. This absorbs some of the energy of the ball into the bat.

Use a bat to draw a semicircle in the dirt about 10 feet (3 m) away from home plate. Have a pitcher or coach stand on the mound and softly toss balls into the strike zone. Batters must try to keep their bunts short enough that the ball stays within the semicircle.

Chapter 4

FIERCE *Infielders*

A strong infield is a key part of a good softball team. These players are excellent fielders and incredible throwers. They also have to be good at communicating and predicting how a runner will behave on the bases.

Throwing Mechanics

Hold the softball in your dominant hand. Lift the ball to just behind your ear. Shift your weight into your back leg. This will be the same side as your throwing arm. Step forward with your front leg, point at your target with your glove or elbow, and extend the ball up and over your head. Release when the ball is in front of you. Snap your wrist down toward the ground as you release the ball.

TRASH CAN *Toss*

~ *Tip* ~

When your team is fielding, always stand in a ready position. Take a wide stance, bend your knees, and bring your hands out in front of your body.

Line up at third base. Set a large garbage can on its side on first base, with the open end pointing towards the infield. Then, have a parent or friend hit a grounder to you. Field the ball and throw it to first base. Your goal in this drill is to throw into the garbage can.

Be Ready to Move

In elite levels, a very fast pitcher can throw the ball around 50 miles (80 kilometers) per hour. A strong batter can send a ball rocketing back into the field at 60 miles (97 km) per hour! The faster infielders can react to a batter's movements, the more likely they will be to field the hit.

Infielders need to be ready for fly balls, line drives, and ground balls. Fly balls are hits that soar high into the air. Line drives are hit in fast, direct lines that don't touch the ground. Grounders are tricky hits because they roll, bounce, and jump across the bumpy ground.

Mechanics of Fielding Grounders

Start in ready position. As soon as you can tell where the ball is headed, get in front of it. If you have time, step or jog forward toward the ball. This is called charging the ball. When you're close enough, bend your knees deeply and bring both hands out in front of you. Keep your glove hand low to the ground and palm up. Hover your bare hand above it. When you catch the ball in your glove, cover it with your bare hand to keep it secure.

FIELDING
Run Throughs

For this drill line up at third base. Have a partner roll the ball to you. Run toward the ball to field it with your glove foot forward and other foot slightly behind. Keep moving your feet! As you grab the ball with your glove, step your throwing foot forward. Then, step with your glove foot as you throw the ball back to the person who rolled it. Work on your steps until you can field and throw the ball in one fluid motion.

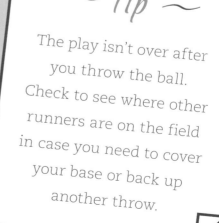

~ Tip ~

The play isn't over after you throw the ball. Check to see where other runners are on the field in case you need to cover your base or back up another throw.

The Dynamic Duo

Every player on a softball team is important. But there are two infield positions that are engaged in every single play: the pitcher and catcher.

Mechanics of a Fast Pitch

Start with both feet touching the pitching rubber. Your glove side foot should be slightly behind your throwing foot. Bring both hands into your chest. As you step forward with your glove-side foot, use your throwing-side leg to push your body forward. At the same time, windmill your throwing arm up and around. Release the ball just as it passes in front of your throwing side thigh.

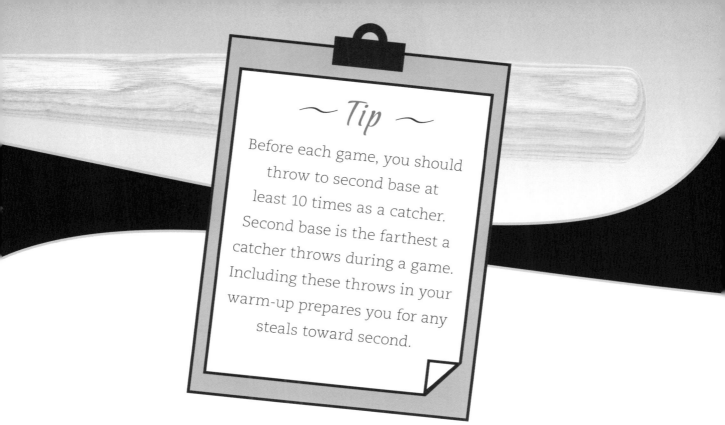

~ *Tip* ~

Before each game, you should throw to second base at least 10 times as a catcher. Second base is the farthest a catcher throws during a game. Including these throws in your warm-up prepares you for any steals toward second.

Mechanics of Catching

Start in a squat position with your feet about shoulder-distance apart. Your weight should be on the inner balls of your feet. Extend your glove out toward the pitcher to give her a good target for her pitch. Let your throwing arm rest down by your side or behind your back. As soon as the pitch is released, shift your weight to keep the center of your body behind the ball. Catch the ball with your glove extended out in front of you.

Chapter 5

OUTSTANDING
Outfielders

Outfielders have a lot of responsibility and even more ground to cover! Each outfielder is responsible for roughly one-third of the outfield. That's more than 100 feet (30 m) from side to side and around 40 feet (12 m) forward and back.

Catching a Fly Ball

Stand in a ready position facing home plate. If the ball is going behind you, take a step back with the foot closest to the ball. This is called a **drop step**. Pivot your hips toward the fence and run with your head turned over your shoulder to watch the ball. When you're ready, position yourself and extend your glove to catch the ball. Ideally, you should always catch a fly ball just above your forehead with your body facing where you're going to throw it. Immediately place your throwing hand on top of your glove to trap the ball.

PARTNER *Toss*

Grab a partner and head out to the outfield. Stand about 5 feet (2 m) apart. Have her toss a short pop up over your shoulder. Drop step towards the ball. Make sure you call out, "MINE!" as soon as you can. Catch the ball and return it to your partner. Do this drill five times for each shoulder and then switch places with your partner.

~ Tip ~

Don't backpedal! Running backward is a bad way to catch a ball, and a good way to fall down.

drop step—a technique used for catching fly balls; to step back with one foot in order to position yourself to catch a fly ball

Throwing the Distance

Outfielders need good arm strength. They may have to throw to a **cutoff** player in the infield or throw all the way to a base. This is no easy task. A throw from the fence to home could be more than 200 feet (61 m) long.

The Mechanics of an Outfield Throw

As soon as you've made your catch, execute a **crow hop**. Shift the glove-hand side of your body at your target. Shift your weight onto your back foot, bring your front leg up, and hop for distance—not height. Your back foot should hit the ground first. As you're doing this, windmill your throwing arm behind your back. Bring your arm up, over, and across the front of your body. Release the ball as your front foot hits the ground again. As you release the ball for your throw, let your momentum carry you forward a couple of steps. Don't hold back! The harder you snap your wrist down, the harder your throw will be.

---

cutoff—a player who receives the ball from the outfield to break up a long-distance throw

crow hop—a jumping step taken at the start of a long-distance throw

Now What?

You're conditioned. You've done your drills. You know your stuff.
Now what? Now it's time to head out onto the field. Try your hardest,
and have fun! Always remember to support your teammates and show
sportsmanship, no matter who wins.

GLOSSARY

conditioning (kuhn-DI-shun-ING)—the act of training the body for top physical performance

crow hop (KROH HOP)—a jumping step taken at the start of a long-distance throw

cutoff (kuht-OFF)—a player who receives the ball from the outfield to break up a long-distance throw

drop step (DROP STEHP)—a technique used for catching fly balls; to step back with one foot in order to position yourself to catch a fly ball

endurance (en-DUR-enss)—the ability to keep doing an activity for long periods of time

inning (IN-ing)—a period in a softball game; each team has the chance to field balls and bat once during an inning

momentum (moh-MEN-tuhm)—the force or speed created by movement

region (REJ-uhn)—an area or district

round (ROUND)—to approach the base at a curved angle, step on the inside corner of the base, and take a couple of steps off the base to see where the ball is

strategy (STRAT-uh-jee)—a plan for winning a competition

strength training (STRENGTH TRAY-ning)—activities that make the muscles stronger

strike zone (STRIKE ZOHN)—the imaginary box in a batter's hitting zone that determines whether a pitch is a ball or a strike; a strike zone is usually above the knees and below the chest

READ MORE

Kenney, Karen Latchana. *Strength Training for Teen Athletes: Exercises to Take Your Game to the Next Level.* North Mankato, Minn.: Capstone Press, 2012.

Rogers, Amy B. *Girls Play Softball.* Girls Join the Team. New York: PowerKids Press, 2016.

Woodyard, Janelle Valido. *A Girl's Guide to Softball.* Get in the Game. North Mankato, Minn.: Capstone Press, 2012.

INTERNET SITES

FactHound offers a safe, fun way to find Internet sites related to this book. All of the sites on FactHound have been researched by our staff.

Here's all you do:
Visit *www.facthound.com*

Type in this code: **9781515747215**

Check out projects, games and lots more at
www.capstonekids.com

INDEX